Baby Journal

Born in April

This book belongs to

• •

This is how

our family

has looked until April 202...

Add a picture here

April

Add a picture here

Little ....is born

Hello World!

Date of birth ....

.... **Weight**

Place of birth ....

.... **Height**

Hour of birth ....

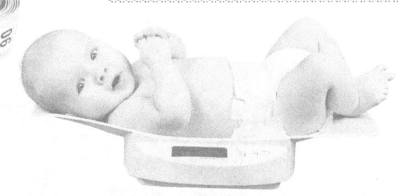

Add a picture here

Weight

Height

May

News of the month

Add a picture here

June

Weight

Height

News of the month

Add a picture here

Weight

Height

July

News of the month

Add a picture here

August

Weight

Height

News of the month

Add a picture here

September

News of the month

Weight

Height

Add a picture here

October

News of the month

Weight

Height

Add a picture here

November

News of the month

○ ─────────────────── ○

○ ─────────────────── ○

○ ─────────────────── ○

○ ─────────────────── ○

Weight

Height

Our first Christmas together

Add a picture here

December

NEWS OF THE MONTH

○———————————————○
○———————————————○
○———————————————○
○———————————————○

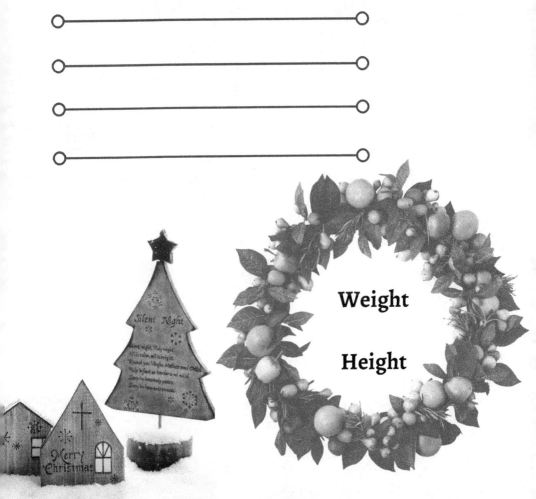

Weight

Height

Add the first picture here

January

Weight

Height

News of the month

Add a picture here

February

News of the month

· ·

· ·

· ·

Weight

Height

Add a picture here

March

News of the month

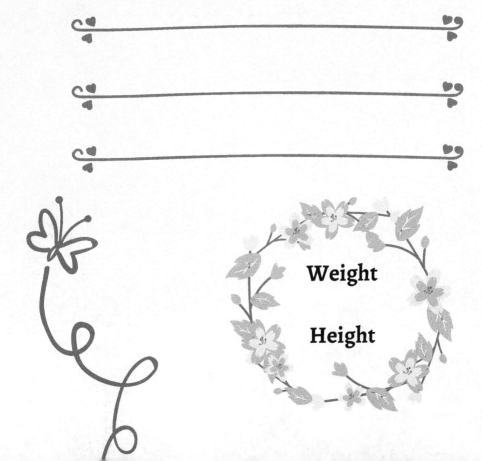

Weight

Height

Happy Birthday, Little Angel!

Add a picture here

April Again

News of the month

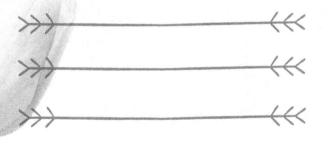

Weight

Height

Add a picture here

Medical Record
Immunizations

Type	Age	Date	Reaction

Add a picture here

The baptism

Date............................

Location....................

Church.......................

Godparents................

Happy birthday, mom!

Add a picture here

Happy birthday, dad!

Add a picture here

Baby's First Times

First Haircut

....

....

First Meal

....

....

Baby's First Times

First Climbing

....

....

First Step

....

....

Baby's First Times

First Calling of MOM

Mom....

:::::::::::::::::::::::::
:::::::::::::::::::::::::

Dad....

First Calling of DAD

·············
·············

Baby's First Times

First Tooth

....

....

First Party

....

....

This is MOM

About My Mother

This is DAD

About My Father

Thoughts

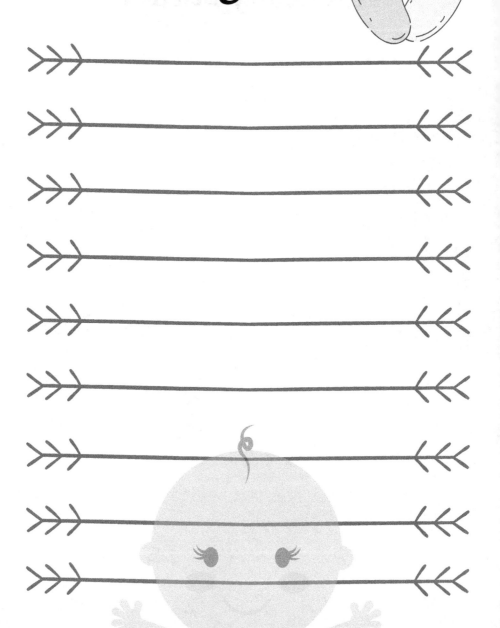

Thoughts

Thoughts

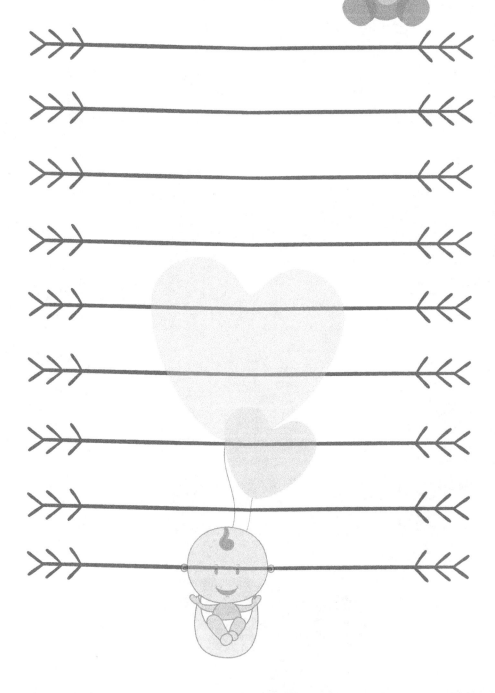

Thoughts

Thoughts

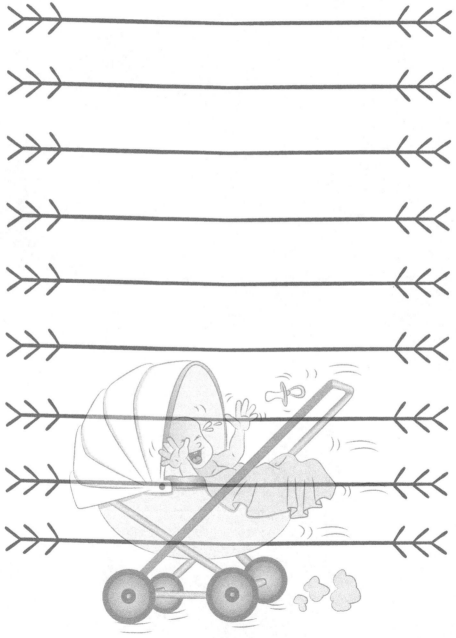

Thoughts

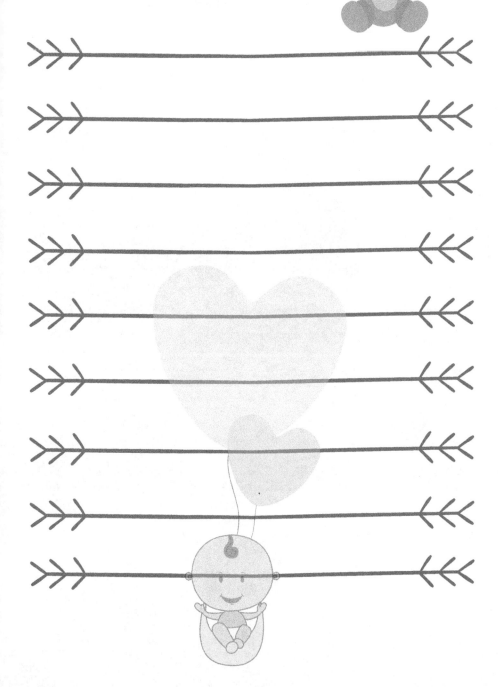

Other Special Moments

Other Special Moments

Other Special Moments

Other Special Moments

Other Special Moments

Other Special Moments

Other Special Moments

Other Special Moments

We hope you enjoyed our book.

As a small family company, your feedback is very important to us.

Please let us know how you like our book at:

book.alina.cooper@gmail.com

CPSIA information can be obtained
at www.ICGtesting.com
Printed in the USA
BVHW091100030521
606332BV00004B/409

9 787557 666743